Insects

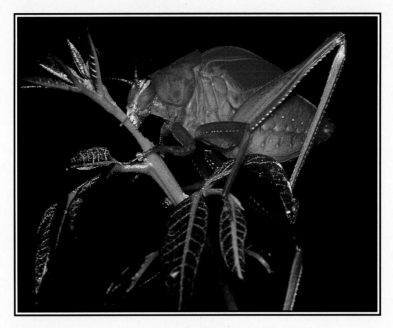

WRITER
Joni Phelps Hunt

SERIES EDITOR
Vicki León

PRINCIPAL PHOTOGRAPHERS
Robert and Linda Mitchell

PHOTOGRAPHERS
Frank Balthis, Gerry Ellis, R. J. Erwin,
Michael Fogden, Jeff Foott, Barbara Gerlach,
John Gerlach, Richard R. Hansen, Stephen J. Krasemann,
Dwight R. Kuhn, Tom and Pat Leeson, Mark Moffett,
Kevin Schafer and Martha Hill, Doug Wechsler,
Larry West, Art Wolfe, Belinda Wright

DESIGNER
Ashala Nicols Lawler

SILVER BURDETT PRESS

© 1995 Silver Burdett Press
Published by Silver Burdett Press.
A Simon & Schuster Company
299 Jefferson Road, Parsippany, NJ 07054
Printed in the United States of America
10 9 8 7 6 5 4 3 2 1

CLOSE-UP
A Focus on Nature

SILVER BURDETT PRESS
© 1995 Silver Burdett Press
Published by Silver Burdett Press.
A Simon & Schuster Company
299 Jefferson Road, Parsippany, NJ 07054
Printed in the United States of America
10 9 8 7 6 5 4 3 2 1

Library of Congress
Cataloging-in-Publication-Data
Hunt, Joni Phelps, 1956-
    Insects: all about ants, aphids, bees, fleas, termites,
toebiters & a beetle or two / by Joni Phelps Hunt; pho-
tographs by Robert and Linda Mitchell.
        p. cm.
Includes bibliographical references and index.
    ISBN 0-382-24878-3 (LSB)
    ISBN 0-382-24879-1 (SC)
    1. Insects–Juvenile literature. [1. Insects.]
I. Mitchell, Robert Wetsel, 1933-   ill. II. Mitchell, Linda,
1944-   ill. III. Title.
QL467.2. H85 1994
595.7–dc20
                                        94-3046
                                            CIP
                                            AC

Insects

Contents

What are insects?

Float like a butterfly, sting like a bee, sing like a grasshopper, work like an ant. Each different, yet all these creatures are insects. Members of this huge group share many traits:

🐜 bodies in three parts – head, thorax, and abdomen ('insect' means 'in segments')

🐜 six jointed legs attached to the thorax; insects are part of a larger group called arthropods or 'jointed foot'

🐜 no internal skeleton; instead, a hard covering or exoskeleton outside the body

🐜 holes in the thorax and abdomen called spiracles to breathe air

🐜 two antennas for smell, touch, and sometimes hearing

🐜 wings: usually two pairs, but sometimes one pair or none

🐜 piercing, sucking, sponging, or chewing mouthparts

An insect's brain connects to a nerve cord that runs down the body. Some insects have chewing mouthparts, like the grasshopper above. Others, like the fly, use a daggerlike stylet to stab prey.

Insects have two kinds of eyes. Simple eyes react to light but can't see images. Compound eyes recognize colors, shapes, patterns, and movement. Take a look at the robber fly on this page. Each of its bright green compound eyes has about 4,000 facets. Each one of those sees a single image. The total picture is formed by many dots – a bit like looking through a magnifying glass at the photographs in this book.

Directly behind the head, the thorax or midsection is where the legs and wings, if any, are attached.

An insect's abdomen is softer and more flexible than its other parts because breathing takes place here. Insects take in air and let it out through holes

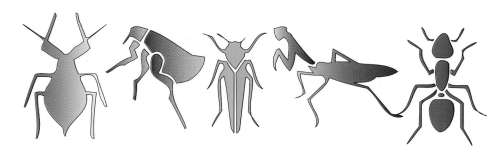

called spiracles. The spiracles lead to a maze of air tubes, which circulate oxygen through the body. This is a primitive system, and if insects grew any bigger, it might not work.

Luckily for us, however, giant ants and monster cockroaches aren't possible. Why? Engineering. Having an external 'suit of armor' instead of a bony skeleton limits the size of insects and other arthropods. ■

Top: *Among the non-insects, the desert millipede curls up tight to avoid being eaten.*

Bottom: *The leg count of the blue tarantula from Laos looks like ten, but the two in front are pedipalps, used as feelers.*

Not all creepy crawly critters are insects

Other arthropods we may think of as insects or 'bugs' also have segmented bodies, jointed legs, and hard external coverings, but scientists classify them differently.

Spiders, scorpions, ticks (Arachnids)
• two body regions
• eight legs
• no antennas
• mouthparts may have pincers or fangs with poison

Crabs, lobsters, shrimps, sow bugs (Crustaceans)
• two body regions
• ten or more legs
• four antennas
• mouthparts may have pincers

Centipedes (name means 100 feet)
• a head and trunk of 15 to 181 segments
• two legs per segment
• two antennas
• may have claws and a venomous bite

Millipedes (name means 1000 feet although no species has that many)
• a head and trunk of nine to 100 segments
• two legs per segment (two segments often fuse together)
• two antennas

All about insects

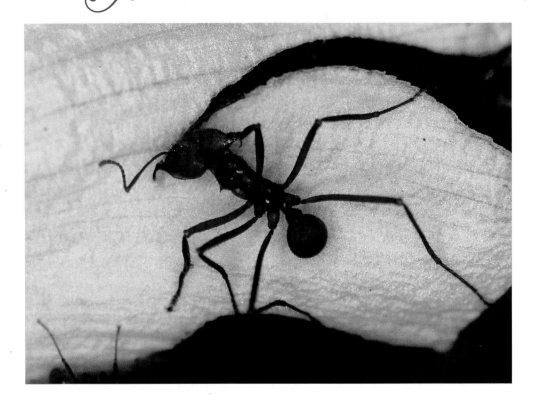

Page 4: *The leaf-cutter ant of tropical America chews off a half-inch piece of leaf to carry back to its nest.*

Page 5: *An assassin bug stabs a bee on its sharp stylet.*

Entomologists, the folks who study insects, tell us there are about 200 million insects for every human being on earth. (At some of the picnics I've been to, it looks like all 200 million of mine have showed up to eat, and they're all ants.)

For such small creatures, insects command large numbers. Some 1½ million species have been identified, and there may be as many as five million more as yet undiscovered. How did so many insects come to exist?

First of all, insects have been around a long time. Their ancestors lived about 395 million years ago – about 165 million years before any dinosaurs.

Secondly, they are masters of survival. Tiny size lets them live and find food in microhabitats, where other animals would starve. Short life spans – usually less than one year – and huge numbers of offspring mean that new generations of insects can adapt quickly to changes in their environments.

Adults and young of the same species often eat different foods. A butterfly and its offspring, the caterpillar, for instance, don't compete for food or habitat. About 300 million years ago, insects developed the ability to fly. Many use wings to migrate to new sources of food or a better climate. Insects have a tough outer covering and other abilities that improve survival. Some can go dormant, others can go without food or water for long periods of time.

Insects are found almost everywhere on earth, including places you might not expect: underground, in the Arctic, in boiling water, in the sky, on and inside other animals – and humans – and on (but not under) the ocean. The largest and most varied insect populations are found in tropical rainforests. Why? Warm temperatures, even climate, and lush plant growth create the perfect conditions.

Although most insects measure half-an-inch long or less, the rainforest produces the world-record holders. From Africa's rainforest comes the goliath beetle, at six inches long and fat as a rat, the heaviest. Longest is the 14-inch giant walking stick of Papua New Guinea. Biggest wingspan goes to the Asian atlas moth, at 12 inches about the size of a small pizza.

Most insects, however, tend to be much less noticeable. The smallest insect fits through the eye of a needle. Called the fairy fly wasp, it lays its eggs inside the eggs of other insects.

The majority of insects pass through similar life cycles. They lay eggs that develop outside the mother's body. After young hatch, most make a change in form, called metamorphosis, to become adults.

Grasshoppers, termites, mantises, and others make an incomplete or simple metamorphosis.

The young, called nymphs, resemble adults with compound eyes and mouthparts, and eat the same foods. To mature, the nymph must grow and develop reproductive organs and wings. As it grows, the nymph sheds or molts its exoskeleton and replaces it with a larger one. Most insects molt four to eight times, each time looking more like an adult. Dragonflies and mayflies also go through incomplete metamorphosis, but their young, called naiads, live in water and don't look or act like adults.

Butterflies, moths, ants, bees, flies, beetles, and others make a complete metamorphosis. Young, called larvas, don't resemble adults in looks or behavior. Larvas can be caterpillars, maggots, or grubs. For the final molt before adulthood, the larva becomes a pupa. Inside its pupal case, it doesn't feed as the body develops into an adult shape with wings, legs, internal organs, and other body parts.

An Io moth shows regular leaflike camouflage, inset photo, and an eyespot startle display, large photo.

The change takes from four days to several months. When complete, an adult emerges.

Most adult insects live several weeks. During that time, their primary instinct is to mate and have off-spring. They use an array of cues to attract mates – everything from a firefly's flashing signal to a cricket's wing chirp to a moth's scent on the wind. Some species have courtship rituals – running, hopping, flying, dancing, or presenting food.

After mating, the female chooses an egg-laying site that has the correct food for her young after they hatch. In some species, the male dies immediately after mating. Generally, insects leave eggs unattended, but there are exceptions. Ants and some bees tend their young. The male giant water bug carries eggs on his back until offspring emerge.

Mouthparts determine whether an insect feeds on plants, animals, or both. The chewing mouthpart works like a jaw with teeth for cutting, crushing, and grinding solid food. Beetles, grasshoppers, and dragonflies have these.

A sucking mouthpart lets insects sip plant juices or body fluids. Butterflies and moths uncoil their strawlike proboscis to drink plant nectar. True bugs, fleas, and some flies have piercing-sucking mouth-parts. They stab prey, inject it with toxins, then suck the prey's internal parts, which have turned to juice. A sponging mouthpart used by some flies soaks up liquid and food.

When threatened, insects fly or scurry for cover where predators can't follow. Others use color and body shape to blend into the background, like the moth in the small photo above. Some use bright colors to advertise their poisons, as with a monarch butterfly. They can also adopt the look of another bad-tasting creature, called Batesian mimicry.

A sudden change in appearance works as a startle display for the moth on page 6. Stink bugs release a skunklike odor; wasps sting. The exoskeleton of beetles acts like armor to repel some invaders. And social insects, like bees, sound an alarm to rally a whole colony to attack.

Insects do useful work on our planet. They pollinate plants, feed on pests that kill plants, serve as food for fishes, birds, and many other animals, and help break down and recycle dead vegetation and animals.

They are also of vital help to humans. Crops and orchards pollinated by insects yield about $19 billion per year in the United States alone. Some insects help control other species considered pests. Bee products, such as honey and bee pollen, give us high-powered nutrition. Beeswax is used in candles, inks, polishes, and cosmetics. Silkworm cultivation, begun in China nearly 4,500 years ago, gives us fabric. Insects contribute to medical research and are used to make shellac, dyes, and drugs. In many countries, insects provide a key source of protein for people.

Biologists estimate that 99 percent of known species are beneficial, or at least not harmful to humans. Just one percent is to blame for damage to crops and property and the transmission of disease. That one percent does, however, pack a punch. Insects in some countries consume as much as half of all the plant crops grown each year. Damage in the U.S. runs about $3 billion annually. An additional $1 billion is lost each year when insects get into grain, building materials, books, and clothing. But blood-sucking insects – mosquitoes, flies, lice, fleas, and others – account for the most havoc. They spread serious diseases, from malaria to yellow fever. More humans have died from these diseases than have been killed in all the wars in history.

Insects have been around much longer than humans. For all our efforts to kill them, we've only succeeded in poisoning our own soil and water. But we're learning. We're trying gentler, smarter strategies.

Farmers and gardeners now partner plants with helpful insect allies. They disrupt mating cycles with pheromones and genetically altered insects. Instead of poisonous chemical pesticides, they use a variety of non-toxic barriers and sprays, from citrus oils to starch. One of the most promising is neem oil, which poisons or repels over 125 difficult pests.

There's still much to learn from these little creatures. Join us for a closeup look at some key players in the pages to come. ■

Top: *This insect-eating robber fly poses as a bee for defense and to surprise prey.*

Bottom: *Wasplike looks allow this moth to avoid predators and feed on flowers during the day.*

Flies

Talk about weird – flies have taste buds in their feet. That's why they stand in their food.

The 100,000 or so species of flies live just about everywhere. They come in all sizes, from fungus flies at less than one-quarter inch to craneflies ten times larger. Their insect order, Diptera, is Greek for two wings, which they move at up to 2,000 beats a second. What once were rear wings have become small knobs that help steady them in flight and make flies the most maneuverable insects around. Add their hairy, sticky feet, and you've got a fly that can land on anything, even glass ceilings.

Fly food favorites are nectar, plant sap, fruit juice, blood, other insects, and decaying matter. A housefly absorbs liquids and food particles with its spongelike mouth, then slurps it up through the proboscis. Bacteria stick to legs and mouthparts and then are transferred at the fly's next stop.

A robber fly hunts prey – flies, wasps, beetles, grasshoppers, butterflies, dragonflies – from a perch. As if it has an on-board computer system, the head tilts and body moves to follow the prey's flight. When speed, trajectory, and distance are computed, the robber fly zooms out to intercept and snag its meal with its legs. The fly stabs prey with the stylet, injects poison, and returns to

its perch. The poison turns the victim's insides to liquid, which the robber fly sucks out.

When looking for a mate, the male robber fly hovers in front of the female, buzzing and moving to let her know it's a partner, not a meal, he's after.

Houseflies lay four or five batches of eggs – over 100 in each – on a food source like garbage, rotting flesh, or dung. Young, called maggots, hatch in a day. Soft and white, without distinct heads or legs, they pupate into adults in ten to 14 days.

The tachinid fly lays eggs in or outside a caterpillar or other animal. The parasite larvas feed on the host and finally kill it as they're ready to become pupas. Tachinid flies control insect populations, second only to wasps.

Flies have many bad points. As one of the world's worst pests, the Mediterranean fruit fly attacks more than 250 kinds of fruits, nuts, and vegetables. Flies spread malaria, yellow fever, sleeping sickness, typhoid, and dysentery.

On the plus side, they help control other insect pests, act as scavengers and recyclers, and serve as food themselves. Many act as pollinators. Syrphidae flies feed on aphids and are second in importance only to bees when it comes to pollination. ◼

Page 8: *Fly pollinates lilies.*
Page 9 top: *Robber fly devours fruit fly;* **bottom,** *tachinid fly lays parasite eggs on caterpillar.*

True bugs

All bugs are insects, but not all insects are bugs – just some 23,000 species. Most live on land, some in water. They range in size from chinch bug nymphs so small you could put two on the head of a pin to a 4½" long "toebiter" bug. Ouch.

What makes these true bugs different? They belong to the Hemiptera order, meaning half wing. The front wings fold flat over the bug's back and cover the shorter rear wings, used to fly. Between the wings is a distinctive triangle-shaped area. Many use strong smells to chase away predators. Some, like the stink bug, wear bright warning colors and patterns.

True bugs have a piercing-sucking mouthpart shaped like a beak. The predators use it to stab insects, small mollusks, tadpoles, or young fish.

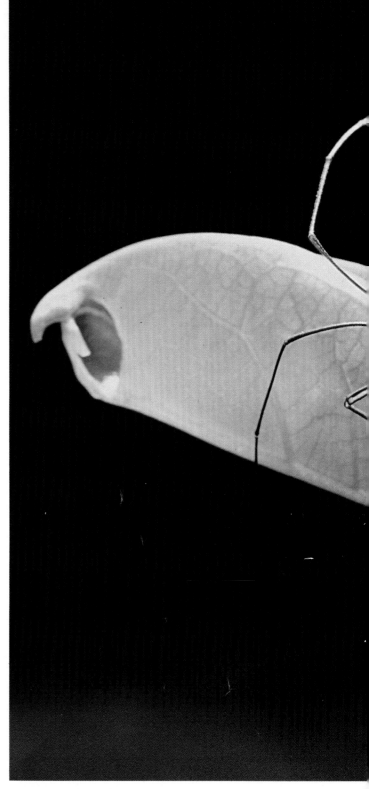

While this dagger at the front of the head holds prey, the bug sucks out body juices. Other true bugs use their stylet only to pierce plants and suck sap. Most sap-suckers are harmless; a few cause severe damage to crops.

The black and white chinch bug is small – three can fit on a penny. But it greedily sucks about $50 million of sap annually from U.S. crops. Adult chinch bugs take cover during winter, then mate and lay eggs in spring. Each female lays 500 tiny amber-colored eggs – about 20 a day – at the base of grain stalks. Over the next one to seven weeks, nymphs hatch and climb the stalks to feed. Several molts and four weeks later, adults with wings appear.

One acre of wheat feeds 15 million of these pests.

Chinch bugs don't stop with one crop. In late June they walk to the nearest corn or oat or barley field, where they suck more sap. In fall, they destroy grasses. Chinch bugs can survive floods, ice, and cold to -20°F. What stops them? Birds, frogs, spiders, ground beetles, and a wasp that lays parasitic eggs.

Among bug predators is the silver-dollar-sized assassin bug. It stalks prey, stabs it, and injects a paralyzing saliva. When the saliva turns the animal's insides to soup, the assassin bug sips its meal. When not used to hunt, its stylet fits into a groove between the bug's front legs.

The ambush bug also makes bug soup. Smaller than a dime, it uses camouflage to hide in a flower.

Page 10: *The coreid bug of Indonesia guards its eggs against predators.*

Pages 10-11: *Two flag-footed bugs in the Costa Rican rainforest mate on a pea pod. Their bright legs distract enemies away from their bodies.*

When a bee, wasp, or butterfly comes to find nectar or pollen, the ambush bug grabs it with strong front legs.

True bugs living in ponds and streams use their legs in unusual ways. A water strider skates across water with four long, skinny back legs. Waxy, waterproof hairs work like snow shoes on the water's surface tension.

The backswimmer spends life floating on its back. For quick moves, it strokes its long, flattened hind legs like oars, with its body acting like a boat. Body hairs trap a layer of air to keep the half-inch bug waterproof. When hairs on the legs feel ripples in the water, a backswimmer rows in that direction to find a tasty insect, tadpole, or small fish. To attract a mate, the male makes noise by rubbing its front legs against its mouthparts.

The slender, 1½"-long water scorpion lives underwater but can't swim well. Instead, it hides in vegetation at the edge of a pond. Two tails at the end of its abdomen form a sort of snorkle that sticks above water while the bug holds onto a plant (upside down) and waits for prey.

A giant water bug, called the toebiter, prefers to feed on small fish, tadpoles, snails, and insects. Sometimes it gets confused and goes after bare feet wading in a pond or stream. Toebiters up to 1½" live in New England, west of the Rockies, and across southern Canada. Toebiters bigger than coffee mugs live in the tropics. The female of some species lays its eggs on the back of the male. After mating, she holds him and sticks the eggs on. He may try to rub them off in vegetation, but they're stuck tight. The male then surfaces to give the eggs the proper balance of oxygen. When the young hatch, the gluelike substance washes off his wings. ■

A male toebiter in Baja California, Mexico, carries unhatched eggs on his back. Some nymphs have already hatched.

Crickets

Chirp, chirp, chirp. We hear them alone or in a chorus. Kin to grasshoppers and katydids, crickets are members of the Orthoptera order, meaning straight wings. About 23,000 species live around the world.

Why do they sing so much? To attract a mate, to claim and defend territory, and to warn others of danger. Sounds, called stridulations, are made by the thin, tough front wings. Over 100 rough ridges under the wing, called a file, rub against a hard scraper on top of the wing to create the chirp. Crickets' short wings have a more high-pitched song than grasshoppers' long ones.

This male cricket lifts his vibrating wings so that his song travels farther to attract a mate.

Each cricket species has a different sound, which speeds up in warm weather and slows in cold. The snowy tree cricket can even tell you the temperature. When you count the number of chirps it makes in 15 seconds and add 37, you'll be close to the temperature in degrees Fahrenheit.

Crickets run from less than one-half inch to almost two inches; a field cricket is under an inch long.

Cricket antennas can double the insect's length. Some also have antenna-like feelers or cerci on the abdomen. Tiny hairs on the cerci catch vibrations in the air or on the ground to help the cricket hear. Its regular "ears" are just below its knees on the front legs.

When a male sings to attract a mate, she moves toward the sound. In some species the female calls back so they can locate each other in the dark. After mating, the female uses her long egg-layer or oviposter to push eggs into soil or a plant stem where they are protected during the winter. A female field cricket lays as many as 300 tiny banana-shaped eggs. Beginning in late spring, nymphs hatch, molt up to a dozen times, and become adults in two to three months.

Both nymphs and adults have chewing mouthparts and feed mainly on plants. Crickets also snack on clothing left in the garden. In turn, crickets serve as a favorite food for larger insects and insect relatives.

Black field crickets like solar-heated homes under a stone. Cave crickets live deep inside caves, where their long antennas serve as eyes in the dark. They have no wings, so they can't sing. Mole crickets burrow in wet sand beside a stream or pond with short, broad front legs that act like shovels.

Tree crickets are beneficial to fruit growers because they eat aphids. But eggs laid in a fruit tree can kill part or all of the tree. In some parts of the world, a cricket's strong jaws are used to remove the tough skin of corns on a person's foot. In Asia, crickets are symbols of good luck. People there keep crickets in cages to enjoy their songs. ■

Mosquitoes

The world's biggest insect troublemaker is the tiny cross-shaped mosquito. It belongs to Diptera, the same order as flies. A mosquito doesn't really bite. Instead, it stabs you with its stylet, injects saliva, and sucks your blood.

It's only the female that acts like a vampire. She needs the protein in bird or mammal blood for her eggs to develop. Without it, she lays far fewer eggs and must digest some of her own wing muscles, thus losing her ability to fly. The male also has piercing and sucking mouthparts, but he feeds on plant juices, dew, and nectar, and helps pollinate wildflowers. When not bearing young, the female feeds on nectar too.

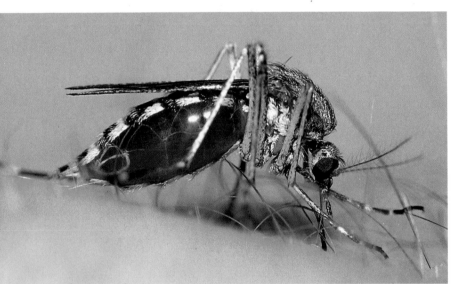

A female mosquito sucks blood from the photographer's arm as food for her eggs.

What are mosquitoes' natural enemies? Birds, bats, mosquito fish, robber flies, and dragonflies. The darner, a dragonfly, with clear wings up to six inches across, zooms through swarms of mosquitoes, captures them with its spine-covered legs, and feeds in midair. With up to 100 mosquitoes in its mouth at once, the darner earns its nickname of mosquito hawk.

A male mosquito uses feathery antennas to hear and find a mate. After doing a courtship dance to attract attention, his antennas vibrate when a female hums her reply. They mate, and the female lays eggs singly or in clusters in water. Eggs of some species stick together to form a raft of 100 to 400. In a few days the eggs hatch into larvas, called wrigglers.

The wriggler moves underwater or hangs upside down just below the water's surface. A tube at the end of its abdomen sticks above water so it can breathe. Hairs next to its mouth push in water loaded with organisms and algae for food. To escape a predator, it contracts and relaxes its muscles to wiggle away.

On its fourth molt, it becomes a pupa or tumbler. Shaped like a comma, the tumbler swims freely, but cannot eat. It needs more oxygen than the wriggler, so it stays close to the surface to breathe through two tubes on its back. After three days, the pupa slowly sheds its skin and emerges as an adult. The mosquito stands on the water until its wings are dried and it can fly. The cycle from egg to adult in warm climates is seven days, longer when cooler.

Mosquitoes are found around water throughout the world in tropical and temperate climates, and even arctic tundra. More of them live in warm climates where they're most dangerous as carriers of disease. A mosquito picks up such diseases as malaria, yellow fever, and encephalitis when she draws blood from wild birds or humans that have the disease. When she has her next meal, she passes on the infection.

The female also carries botfly eggs, a parasite

Mosquito eggs hatch into larvas in the Costa Rican rainforest.

for humans. A botfly captures the mosquito, lays a dozen eggs on the mosquito's legs or abdomen, then lets it go. When the mosquito lands, the person's body heat causes the botfly eggs to hatch. The larvas burrow under the person's skin.

In western lands, we use drainage, insecticides, and other methods to keep mosquitoes under control. Countries with fewer resources aren't so lucky. Each year, malaria attacks about 500 million Asians, Africans, South Americans, and others. In Africa alone, nearly one million kids die of it annually. ■

Fleas

With 1,600 species, there must be a different flea for every kind of dog! Part of the Siphonaptera order, a flea measures less than one-quarter inch and has a narrow body to slide through the hairs of many animals. Extra-long legs give it strength to leap at least a foot into the air – like a human jumping 700 feet. Like mosquitoes, fleas have piercing stylets to suck blood and transmit disease. In 14th-century Europe, fleas spread bubonic plague, or Black Death, from rats to humans. ■

Bees & wasps

How many flowers must bees visit to make one pound of honey? More than two million. Bees and wasps belong to the Hymenoptera order with 108,000 species. Scientists believe this is the most advanced insect group because some species work together to raise young. Ants also belong to this group.

As the major pollinator of plants, bees make an important link in the food chain. Over 150 agricultural crops and countless wild plants depend on bees. Wasps help limit insects by laying their eggs on them. When the eggs hatch, the larvas feed as parasites on the hosts and kill them.

Bees are black or brown with yellow, white, gold, or orange stripes. They can be as long as the word Bees in the title on this page or as small as this H. Wasps average about an inch long, but some spider wasps equal a Tootsie roll in length. The fairy fly wasp is smaller than the period at the end of this sentence. Most also have warning colors of orange or yellow.

Both bees and wasps have chewing and sucking mouthparts. Bees sip nectar from flowers. Their hairy bodies gather sticky grains of pollen, which they also feed on. Female bees often have a basket formed by spines on their rear legs to carry pollen to their nest. Wasps are less hairy and collect less pollen. They also feed on nectar and pollen.

To save energy gathering food, honeybees specialize. To find nectar and pollen, they fly to one type of flower on 97 out of 100 trips. They also prefer the same flower bed. Honeybees gather pollen from the bottom up on spiky flowers and from the outside edge to the center on flat ones.

Bodies of bees and wasps look different from other insects because of their narrow waist. The first part of their abdomen is a flexible joint. They can move easily and quickly to lay eggs, defend themselves, and turn in small nests. Most bees and wasps have four wings; a few like the female velvet ant wasp have none. Their wings move up to 200 beats per second. As the wingbeat slows or speeds, the buzz changes pitch.

Most bee species are solitary, meaning they don't work together to raise young. A male chooses a flower patch and buzzes about, defending it against other males and insects coming to feed. He allows a female to feed and then mates with her.

Afterward the female digs a nest more than a foot deep with an entrance the width of a pencil. Off the main tunnel are rooms or cells. The female combines pollen and nectar into a hard, pea-sized ball, places it in a cell, and lays an egg on it. She closes that cell and moves to the next until the nest is filled with eggs. She seals the nest and leaves the eggs to hatch, feed on pollen, molt, and emerge as adults.

Solitary wasps also build underground cells. One type, called the tarantula hawk, paralyzes a tarantula and drags it into the nest. The wasp lays eggs on the live spider, which becomes food when young wasps hatch. Solitary bees and wasps don't stay to raise their young but leave food for them. This behavior is less evolved than social

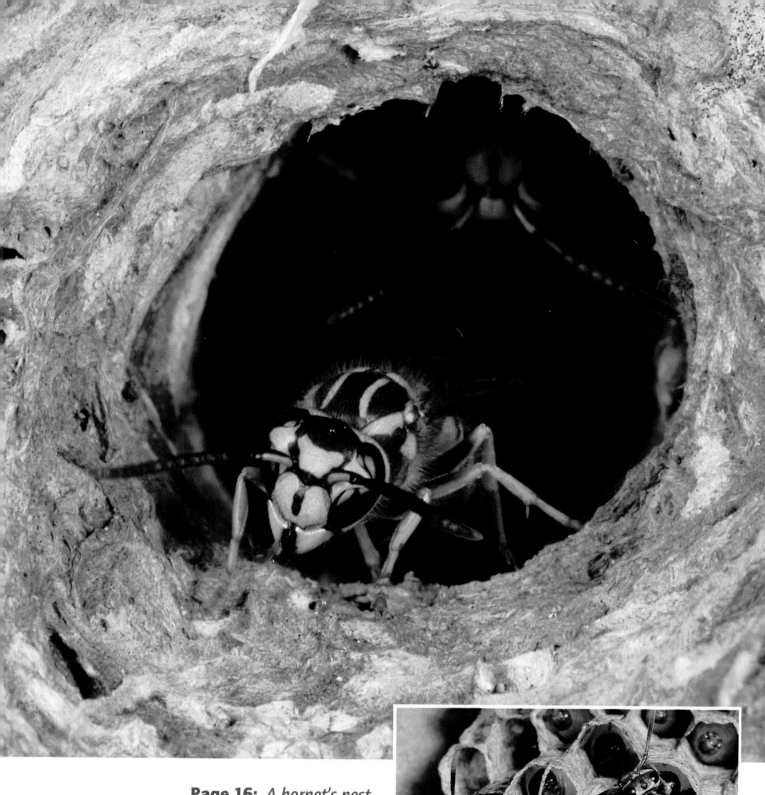

Page 16: *A hornet's nest hangs high in a maple tree.*

Page 17 top: *Yellow jackets peer out of their underground nest;* **bottom,** *paper wasps tend larvas and pupal cells.*

behavior, where adults cooperate to feed and care for young.

Honeybees and bumblebees that make and store honey are social. They live in colonies with one queen, female workers that don't lay eggs, and male drones. Workers build the hive with wax, a fatty substance from glands in their abdomen,

Her pollen basket loaded, a honeybee visits a field poppy.

and care for eggs, larvas, and pupas. They gather pollen and mix it to feed larvas. Without pollen, there can be no new workers, and the colony starves.

Some researchers believe honeybees dance to tell co-workers where to find pollen and nectar. A speedy round dance means food is within

330 feet of the hive. A figure-eight dance means it's farther. The honeybee wiggles its abdomen to show amount, distance, and direction of the food.

When flowers bloom in spring, a queen honeybee mates with a drone. He dies, and she starts a new colony. Several days later she begins to lay eggs. A queen may live five years and lay up to 2,000 eggs daily. Eggs hatch in three days, and workers feed all larvas a white paste called royal jelly. The paste comes from a gland near the worker's mouth. When a female larva is fed this for three days, she becomes a worker; for six days, a queen. After five molts and five or six days, workers close cells with wax while larvas change to pupas. About two weeks later, bees emerge. The new queens leave the colony with several drones to start new hives.

While most insects burrow underground during winter, honeybees huddle inside the hive. Those in the middle begin to "dance," and the heat they generate warms the group. The center can be as much as 75°F warmer than air outside the hive. Bees on the outside of the group slowly work their way into the center and take a turn vibrating their wing muscles. By feeding on the supply of honey, bees have energy to stay warm all winter. A colony of 50,000 bees needs about 50 pounds of honey for the winter.

What's honey and how's it made? It starts as sugar solution or nectar a bee takes from plants. In its honey stomach, the bee adds enzymes to chemically change it. This unripe honey is put into cells in the wax honeycomb and fanned by bees' wings to evaporate water. What's left becomes honey.

Wasps don't make honey, but they show social behavior. Hornets and yellow jackets are similar to bees with one queen, female workers, and male drones. To begin a colony, the queen peels fibers from dry wood or paper with her mouthparts. She mixes these with water and saliva to make six-sided cells. The queen raises the first group of young

Top: *A bee transfers stored flower nectar to a worker in the hive before going out to collect more;* **bottom,** *honey in the comb.*

until workers begin building and nursemaid chores. Instead of collecting pollen for larvas, worker wasps hunt caterpillars and flies.

Many other wasp species are parasites. Usually about the size of a rice grain, adult braconid wasps feed on flower nectar and honeydew from aphids. After mating, a female chooses the host for her eggs, such as a caterpillar. She sticks her needlelike egg-layer under its skin and leaves one or more eggs. Larvas hatch and feed on the host's tissues and body fluids. If vital organs aren't disturbed, the host continues to feed itself and the larvas. When larvas are ready to change to pupas, they eat through the host's skin, killing it.

Predators of larvas and honey include raccoons, skunks, brown bears, hedgehogs, and tiny parasites. The metallic green cuckoo wasp flies into a bee nest, lays an egg, and flies out. When hatched, the larva feeds on stored pollen and bee eggs.

Most female bees and wasps sting, using their sharp egg-layer to defend the nest. Since the stinger and part of the bee's body remain in the victim, the bee soon dies. One wasp can alert a whole colony to attack. Yellow jackets, hornets, and paper wasps have especially painful stings. What about Africanized honeybees or "killer bees"? Their sting is no worse than a honeybee's, but they attack in larger groups, so the victim gets more venom. Scientists fear these bees will interfere with the beekeeping industry and domestic honeybees that pollinate crops. To stop Africanized bees, researchers are replacing their queens with domestic ones. ■

Top: *Known as a fierce predator, a female bordered mantis eats her mate.*

Bottom: *The orchid mantis mimics a flower to protect itself and to startle and grasp unsuspecting prey.*

The mantis Why is that flower moving?

Because it's a mantis in disguise. Found throughout the world, some 1800 species belong to the group Mantodea. The name mantis, meaning prophet in Greek, was chosen because it holds its front legs up in a prayerful gesture.

Two- to four-inches long, the slender praying mantis might well be called "preying" mantis. One of the few insects with a head that turns almost completely around, a mantis lies hidden and closely watches prey. Its strong, spiny front legs dart out to clamp around a meal. Biting mouthparts pierce the back of the head and cut nerves in butterflies, moths, true bugs, caterpillars, wasps, and more. A large mantis may feed on lizards, frogs, and small birds in the same way. Farmers and gardeners welcome the mantis; on a good day it can kill nearly 100 insect pests.

In late summer, males seek a mate. In some species, the male must hold a female so she cannot reach him with her legs or jaws. If he fails to, she grabs him and bites his head off. His body becomes nourishment for her future young. Because nerve centers are located in several parts of its body, a mantis can lose its head and still function. A headless male can raise his wings, walk, or continue to mate. A headless female can continue to lay eggs.

A female makes a mass of soft, sticky foam and lays up to 350 eggs in the center. Placed on plant stems, twigs, or a building, the foam hardens to an inch-long, water-repellent case, called an ootheca. Eggs spend the winter inside and wiggle out as nymphs in late spring or early summer. They're hungry, too. Unless nymphs find aphids or other food quickly, they feed on their brothers and sisters.

A mantis uses camouflage to protect itself. If that doesn't work against birds, small mammals, and reptiles, it lifts and swipes with its jagged front legs. It may also escape by flying away. In Kenya, one species of female mantis guards her egg case from attacks until the eggs hatch. ■

Leaf & stick insects

Like a cartoon, a broken twig comes to life – in slow motion. A stick insect, or walking stick, stays nearly invisible in its plant-filled home. Unlike a mantis that also hides to surprise and capture prey, a stick uses camouflage for defense.

Leaf and stick insects belong to the Phasmatodea order. Many of these plant-eaters average three or four inches, but the giant walking stick of Papua New Guinea measures 14! Some species have two pairs of wings and are quite good flyers.

A stick insect can change color from its usual green, brown, or gray when there's a change in humidity, light, or temperature, or when its habitat is crowded. It may stay still all day, moving only after dark to feed on a leaf. A leaf insect copies a real leaf in shape, color and pattern. There may even be insect damage or decay on the outer covering. To further the illusion, it hangs from a twig by two or three legs and turns slowly, like a leaf blowing in the wind.

Sticks don't gather in hives like bees. They're spread out, so it's harder to find mates. After a male and female do mate, the female drops eggs from her tree home down through leaves to the ground. In spring, the young hatch at night as nymphs and climb into a tree for protection. Some stick and leaf females can produce eggs without mating. For these species, males have not been identified and may not even exist. ■

A female insect called 'beautiful moving leaf' blends into Malayan rainforest leaves.

Grasshoppers & kin

Meet the gold medalists of the insect world. If grasshoppers held Olympic track meets, you'd see them long jump the equivalent of 500 feet or more. Grasshoppers share these abilities with katydids, locusts, and crickets, all members of the 23,000-species Orthoptera order. They live in nearly every habitat – desert to rainforest to mountain range.

To be a champion jumper, a grasshopper has powerful muscles in its long back legs. A fast and high leap helps avoid predators, such as the chameleon, mantis, and digger wasp. Birds and lizards learn to stay away from a brightly colored grasshopper because it's likely poisonous. One grasshopper species oozes bubbles of fluid that cause blisters.

A grasshopper's sturdy, narrow front wings cover its body. Larger, more delicate back wings are used for flying and fold like a fan under the front pair. Some species fly well. Others with short wings don't. Species living in caves are wingless.

Grasshoppers have chewing mouthparts and feed mostly on plants. Those that live underground or in buildings may scavenge for dead insects. They range in size from the length of the icon at the top of this page to the length of the word Grasshoppers in the heading.

A long-horned grasshopper has thin antennas longer than its body. Its two eardrums, called tympanums, sit on its front legs below the knee joint. Home can be in dense shrubs or trees, in meadows, or in plants by streams. For protection, it often mimics a leaf or part of a plant. Long-horns, especially katydids, are known for noisy songs.

A short-horned grasshopper has sturdy antennas less than half its body length. Its eardrums are on the sides of its abdomen. Most live in dry grass-lands and deserts.

Grasshopper calls are most often made by males looking for a mate. Each species has a different call, so a female answers only if he's singing her song. A short-horn makes a low buzz, like running a comb across your fingernails. He rubs rough, toothlike points on his back leg across the front wing's hard edge, or scraper. Long-horns rub ridges on one front wing against the scraper on the other to make a noise like rubbing sandpaper.

As a female moves closer, the male switches to a softer courtship song. After mating, a long-horned female lays eggs on a plant. The short-horned female puts from eight to 100 eggs in a sticky gel into the soil. She lays up to ten clusters, which hatch into nymphs in three or four weeks. Nymphs molt five times during the next two months before they get wings and become adults.

"Kay-tee-did. Kay-tee-did-n't." Three pulses, then four. With its large, bright green wings showing veins and blotches, a katydid imitates the leaf of a tree or shrub where it lives. This three-inch grasshopper, also called a bush cricket, uses its long antennas to smell. Katydids feed on plants.

Short-horned migratory locusts, one of the worst insect pests, devour plants and crops near deserts of Africa, Europe, Asia, South America, and Australia. In years with little rain, the population stays small. Wet weather means more eggs hatch, and more nymphs must compete for food. Their body changes color and grows bigger. They move in large crowds, feeding as they go. When the last molt gives them wings, billions of locusts fly with the wind in huge dark clouds. One swarm in Morocco measured 155 miles long and 12 miles wide. ■

Page 23: *Redlegged grasshoppers gather on teasel.*

Beetles

What is success in Nature's terms? To be a beetle. One out of every four animal species on earth is. With more than 300,000 species, they make up 40 percent of all the world's insects. You know them as june bugs, potato bugs, ladybugs, fireflies, scarabs, and more. They belong to the order Coleoptera, meaning sheath wings. You can find them everywhere except the polar caps and in the sea.

Most beetles can fly short distances, but they usually prefer to crawl around in vegetation. They keep their rear wings, which carry them in the air, sheathed under the leathery or hard front wings, called elytra. When closed, the front wings come together in a straight line down the back.

Beetles have a complete metamorphosis that often happens entirely underground. Their life span runs from a few weeks to several years for some species of wood-boring beetles. With chewing mouthparts, they feed on plants and other insects. Some species destroy crops and forests. Others infest stored food, clothing, and carpets. On the helpful side, the tiger, diving, ladybird, and ground beetles prey on such pests as caterpillars, aphids, and mosquitoes. As scavengers, beetles also clean the environment of dead animals and plants.

Weevils, the largest group of beetles with 40,000 species, have some of the smallest members – you'd need a magnifying glass to see them – and others that reach two inches. A weevil's beak can be nearly as long as its body. The beak has mouthparts at the tip and antennas midway. All weevils feed on plants. To lay eggs, a female bores a hole into stems, fruits, or seeds. After hatching, the larva feeds on its birth plant. Larvas of the boll weevil, originally from Mexico, have caused millions of dollars in damage to U.S. cotton crops.

Stag beetles are named for the male's huge mouthparts, which look like a deer's antlers. Also known as a pinching bug, it uses the powerful pincers for defense and combat with other males to win females. A stag beetle may feed on sap from plants. It can range from the size of a thumbtack up to three inches and often lives in rotting wood, which its larvas eat.

The family known as scarabs includes hercules, Japanese, rhinoceros, dung, and june beetles. Many have brilliant metallic colors. Averaging two inches, a scarab's front legs are wide and often spiked for digging. Tips of its antennas open up for a better sense of smell. At up to seven inches, the male hercules beetle has fearsome-looking horns, but it's harmless. Japanese beetles attack 275 kinds of plants. Other scarabs scavenge food at night as they recycle carrion, dung, and dead plants.

The well-named dung beetle finds fresh manure and rolls it into a ball with its back legs. The beetle digs a hole, buries a dung ball, crawls in the hole, and feeds on it. At the start of mating season, two dung beetles may roll and bury a ball together. The female reshapes it like a pear and lays an egg inside the top. When the egg opens, the larva begins eating, turns into a pupa, and crawls out as an adult.

Page 24: *Two male Western Hercules beetles fight to defend territory and win a mate.*

Page 25 top: *A female blister beetle lays a cluster of eggs;* **bottom,** *a weevil from Papua New Guinea spars with an ant.*

Page 26: *A stag beetle opens its wing case and prepares for takeoff.*

Page 27 left: *One of the scarab family, this hercules beetle has a large horn on its head and a smaller one on its thorax;* **right**, *beetles often come in metallic colors, like this golden scarab.*

Attracted to lights in a house, the nocturnal june beetle or june bug often crashes into window or door screens. A female lays her eggs near the base of herbs, shrubs, and trees. The larvas burrow in the soil, feed on roots, and change to pupas. When they return to the surface as adults, june beetles burrow during the day and come out to feed on leaves at night.

Another nighttime beetle – the firefly or lightning bug – gives a light show in backyards, meadows, and near woods or streams. Its light comes from an enzyme mixing with a chemical called luciferin in the back of the abdomen. A few

lakes, and marshes in spring and summer. It swims with its body half out of water. To watch for predators and prey, it uses eyes like bifocals. Half can see above water and half below. Its antennas also feel ripples in the water to find insect prey. A whirligig can be as small as a rice grain or as large as a dime, and usually stays in a group. It strokes its paddlelike middle and back legs to scoot through the water at 40 inches a second. When disturbed, the beetle whirls around in small circles. Before diving to escape danger, a whirligig takes air under its hard front wings. Once on the bottom, it holds onto an object with its legs. When it lets go, it bobs back to the surface.

The darkling beetle that lives in deserts has found a way to keep from overheating. It's covered with a light-colored waxy coating. This wax is made by special cells under the exoskeleton and is produced from what it eats. The wax reflects several hundred times more sunlight than its regular black coat, so the beetle stays cooler and hunts food longer on the hot desert sands. Many other darkling beetles scavenge at night.

Like many species, the bombardier beetle uses chemicals as a defense against the mantis, birds, and lizards. The tiny bombardier mixes two chemicals stored in its body to create a boiling hot and smelly gas, which it aims and shoots at its attacker with a popping sound. Its cousin, the blister beetle, relies on contact to discourage. Touch it, and a toxin in its joints gives you a blister. ■

other insects give off light, but only fireflies turn it on and off in a pattern. Some flashes last five seconds. Others blink 40 times a second. The number of flashes, time between signals, and brightness are used by the male to attract a female of the same species. While he flies around signaling, she stays in one place and flashes a reply. They alternate signals until they find each other and mate. A few females mimic signals of other species to attract a male. When he lands, she grabs and eats him. Both adult and larva fireflies feed on other insects.

The shiny black whirligig beetle lives in ponds,

Ladybugs

Everyone knows and loves the ladybug, also called the ladybird beetle. Why is this shiny, round, red-orange darling with the black polka dots everyone's insect friend? For gardeners and farmers, the ladybug is one champ bad-bug chomper. More than 3,000 ladybug species in the order Coleoptera feed on pests: aphids, scale insects, mites, and mealybugs.

Kids have always loved ladybugs. An old children's rhyme says: "Ladybug, ladybug fly away home/Your house is on fire, and your children do roam. Except little Nan, who sits in a pan/Weaving gold laces as fast as she can."

The first verse refers to a ladybug that feeds on aphids in the grape vineyards of Europe. After the harvest, the vines are burned. In the second verse, 'little Nan' is one of her children, a larva getting ready to become a pupa. Nan sits on a leaf, making a mat of golden silk that she clings to during her change into an adult.

A ladybug has the basic characteristics of other beetles. In flight, its small back wings beat from 75 to 91 times a second. Its body, the size of the icon at the top of the page or smaller, has chewing mouthparts and short antennas, and it goes through complete metamorphosis.

In all stages of life – adult, larva, pupa – a ladybug wears bright colors and rarely hides from predators. An adult oozes smelly yellowish liquid from its leg joints that its enemies can smell, but

we can't. One species of cockroach in Philippine jungles mimics the shape, size, and color of ladybugs to warn off insect-eating birds. The assassin bug, one of the few ladybug predators, stabs its beak into the beetle's body and sucks out juices.

The life cycle of a ladybug takes just a few weeks. A female puts about 200 eggs (up to 1,000 for one species) in a crevice of tree bark or on the back of a leaf. When hatched, the larva looks like a tiny purplish lizard with red, blue, and black spots. Called an aphid-wolf, the larva feeds constantly – about 40 aphids an hour. It drains the aphid's body juices, and eats the shell. As it grows and molts, the larva also devours scale insects, eggs of potato beetles, and more.

The larva becomes a pupa with a shiny, spotted surface. The winged adult emerges from the pupa hungry for aphids and others, but it needs less food than as a larva.

In cool fall climates, huge clumps of ladybugs cluster together in forest debris, haystacks, under bark on dead trees, under eaves of buildings – anywhere they'll be sheltered from the cold. A supergroup found in a canyon at 4,000-foot elevation was estimated to contain 750 million ladybugs. ■

Ladybugs mass together for warmth and protection in cold climates.

The mayfly

The ancient Greeks gave the mayfly the name ephemeros – "to live but a day." As an adult, it may live a few hours to a few days. About 1500 species form the order Ephemeroptera. With dragonflies and damselflies, they've been around a long time. Ancestors of all three are among the oldest insect fossils found.

A mayfly larva, called a naiad, lives in water. It doesn't look or act like an adult mayfly. A naiad lives up to three years and can molt up to 20 times. With chewing mouthparts, it feeds on plants, algae, or organic matter scavenged in the ponds, streams, or rivers. The naiad has antennas, eyes, gills along the sides of its body to breathe, and three long slender tails.

Usually a naiad is small, but a few reach two inches. It may live in a tunnel it digs with tusklike mouthparts in the soft debris at the bottom of a pond. Or it may swim freely, often quickly, through the water. Naiads in swift rivers crawl along the riverbed and cling to stones or other objects.

A mayfly naiad goes through an extra stage no other insect does to become an adult. It stops feeding, swims to the surface, and has its last molt.

What emerges is a grayish-brown subimago or dun. It has dull-colored wings fringed with hairs, no mouthparts, and short legs. The dun flies from the water to a dry rock or plant. After a few hours, it molts again to become a true adult. As an adult, its large front wings are now shiny and clear and the back wings small or not there at all. Again, the yellowish or brownish adult has no mouthparts and cannot feed.

Millions of mayflies turn into adults at the same time during warm weather in spring and summer. As soon as their wings are ready to fly, males swarm in a frantic mating dance, making loops through the air to attract females. Mating takes place in midair, and males die immediately after. Females go below water to lay eggs on plants and die soon after.

The major predators for both naiads and adults are fish. The insects' only defense are their huge numbers. Fish feed until they're full and leave the rest alone. Many lures used by fly-fishermen are made to look like mayflies. ■

This subimago has wings but will molt once more to become an adult.

Dragonflies

Like miniature helicopters, dragonflies and damselflies zip around ponds, streams, or lakes. They zoom at speeds up to 35 mph, turn in an instant, hover, and even fly backwards. Both dragonflies and damselflies belong to the Odonata order of 5,500 species. Along with mayflies, they're among the oldest flying insects, with fossils dating back 300 million years. Some of their ancestors had wingspans of 30 inches. Today it's three to four.

Slender, often with vivid colors, a dragonfly can be the size of a penny up to five inches. Long, clear wings are reinforced at the base for more power. The head moves in all directions to track prey 40 feet away. Huge compound eyes have up to 50,000 separate lenses that nearly cover a dragonfly's head and bulge on the sides of a damselfly's. Long legs,

not used for walking, are lined with sharp spines. The first two pair bend to make a basket that scoops up and traps flying insects. Sharp mouthparts cut prey into bite-sized morsels.

A dragonfly's voracious appetite makes it quite helpful to humans. During its lifetime of up to three years, it gobbles millions of black flies and mosquitoes, earning the name mosquito hawk. In 30 minutes, a dragonfly can eat its own weight in food. It sits on a perch and darts out to grab prey. Or it can track and catch a meal in mid-flight.

How does a dragonfly maneuver faster than its speedy prey? By being different. Insects usually link the front and back wings on each side of their body to move together. The dragonfly instead moves the front set together and the back together. In flight, a dragonfly twists the wing surface to increase lift and speed. The U.S. military has even studied the way dragonfly wings work for clues to faster flight.

A male dragonfly stakes out territory around water, hoping to attract a female. Everyday he perches on the same stick or rock and watches other males. He may patrol the area, flying a rambling course before returning. If another male enters his turf, the chase begins. He may run the intruder out. They may face off and then chase each other around the area. Or they may zip and zoom like pilots in an aerial dogfight, crashing their wings together.

These activities attract a female's attention. When she enters the area, the male who won the fight displays his bright body colors and patterns. They mate in flight, curled together almost in the shape of a heart. The female lays up to 800 eggs in small clusters underwater or on a water plant's stem. Meanwhile, the male may hover to protect her from other males. When done, the female flies away, and the male returns to patrol his territory.

About a week later the adults die, and the eggs hatch into tiny naiads, which live entirely in water. Like a jet-propelled boat, a naiad draws water into its abdomen, removes the oxygen to breathe, and shoots out a jet of waste water. In this way it darts around the pond after food and away from frogs, water beetles, and other predators.

A naiad grows to more than 20 times its original length – the size of a penpoint – as it feeds constantly on mosquitoes and other insects, tadpoles, and small fish. Its long bottom lip, a labium, has two flat plates hinged together with pincers to grasp prey. The labium stays under the head like a triangular mask until it shoots forward to snatch a meal.

After at least ten molts and up to three years, the brown naiad crawls out of the water at night to a nearby plant or rock. Several hours later the exoskeleton splits open, and an adult struggles out. By morning its wings are dry and strong enough to fly to woods or fields near the pond to feed. There the dragonfly tries to avoid predators – birds, snakes, frogs, and spiders.

How can you tell a damselfly from a dragonfly? Damselflies are smaller, averaging one to two inches. They fly more slowly and with less power. It usually holds its wings up in the air and angled back over its body. A dragonfly rests with its wings stretched out to the side. Neither can fold wings flat against their backs like beetles and true bugs can. ∎

Pages 30 and 31: *Dragonfly wings may look fragile, but they're the most powerful among insects. These wings shimmer with dew.*

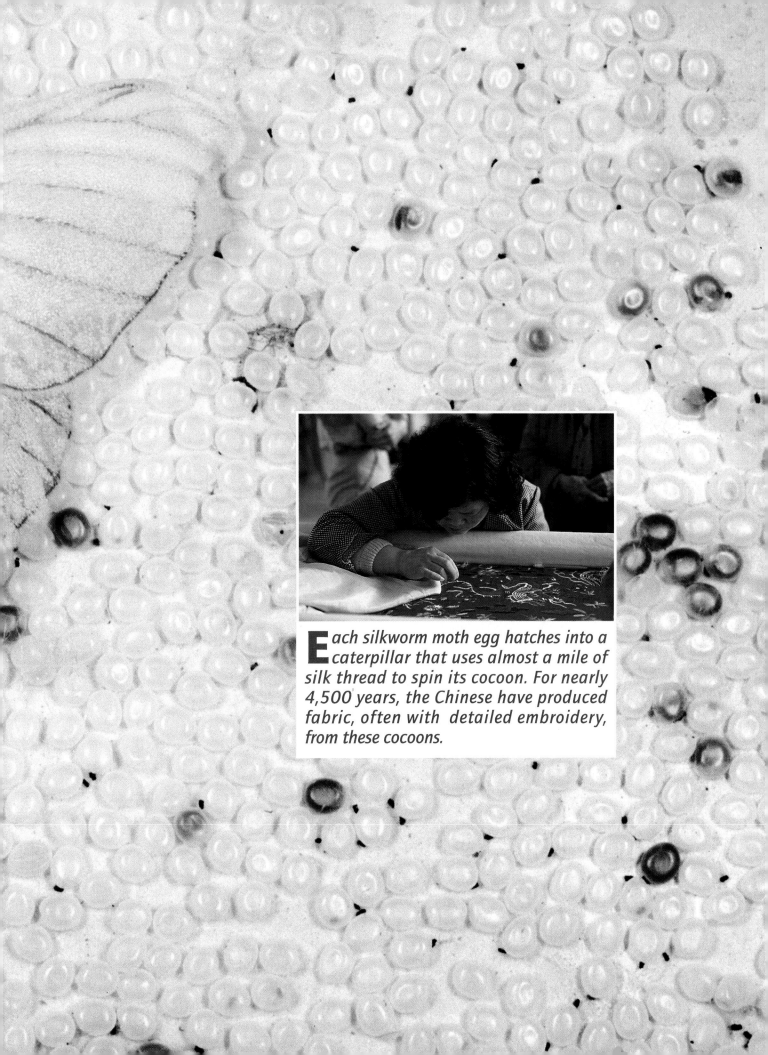

Each silkworm moth egg hatches into a caterpillar that uses almost a mile of silk thread to spin its cocoon. For nearly 4,500 years, the Chinese have produced fabric, often with detailed embroidery, from these cocoons.

Butterflies & moths

Butterflies and moths are Lepidoptera, which means "scale wing." Short, scalelike hairs on the wings overlap like shingles on a roof. What gives wings color? Pigments provide scales with yellow, orange, red, black, gray, and brown. Vivid blues, violets, and iridescent greens come from the way light hits the wing and reflects, similar to colors on a hummingbird. Wings are delicate, and even a gentle rub removes thousands of scales. Of the more than 165,000 Lepidoptera species, moths account for about 145,000. They're found all over the world, except the polar caps and icy mountains.

How to tell if the creature flitting by is a moth or a butterfly? Several cues help. Butterflies usually fly by day, show bright colors, and have knobs at the end of their antennas. They hold wings above their body at rest. Most moths fly at night, show generally muted colors, and have pointed, often feathery antennas. They stretch their wings out flat when still.

The smallest butterfly, the half-inch pygmy blue, lives in California. The largest, nearly 12 inches, is the Queen Alexandra birdwing of Papua New Guinea. The world's largest flying insect? The atlas moth in Asia spreads its wings a full foot.

Lepidoptera that lived 130 million years ago all had chewing mouthparts. Over time, as the amount of flowering plants on Earth increased, most species changed to a sucking mouthpart called a proboscis. Like a straw, this hollow tongue stays

curled beneath the head until it uncoils to sip flower nectar. A few moths still have chewing mouthparts to munch pollen.

What may seem like a butterfly's carefree, zigzag flight actually has purpose. It helps elude predators: birds, bats, monkeys, spiders, beetles, dragonflies, and more. It also helps find a mate and produce young quickly. Some butterflies live only a week. A few species live up to ten months, but the average is two to three weeks. Some male butterflies scatter a scent, or pheromone, to attract females as they fly. With moths, it's the female that spreads perfume from glands in her abdomen. A male silk moth's feathery antennas can pick up scent and find her from nearly three miles away.

A short courtship may include a dance or chase and ends with the two mating, often in the air. The female lays from several dozen to 1,500 eggs on a specific plant that becomes food when the eggs hatch. The time to hatch can take from two days to one year, but the average is about a week.

The larva of a butterfly or moth, called a caterpillar, eats twice its weight in food on the first day. It molts four or five times, nearly doubles in size each time, and ends up about 1,000 times its original weight. A caterpillar looks nothing like the butterfly or moth it will become. It has simple eyes, short antennas, and strong jaws to chew on plants. Instead of six legs, it has

16 - six jointed and up to ten unjointed prolegs. Instead of soaring through the air, it ripples along.

To avoid being a meal for frogs, birds, lizards, wasps, and ants, caterpillars come in all colors and shapes. Some use disguises to look like a snake, a dead leaf, or bird droppings. Others have sharp, poisonous spines or a furry coat. Bright colors outside warn of poisons inside.

How does a caterpillar become a butterfly? It spins a small pad of silk on a leaf or twig and hooks on. It molts one more time, leaving a pupa or chrysalis. A moth caterpillar spins a cocoon around itself from silk glands in its mouth. The outside of a cocoon can be disguised as a twig, leaf, flower, rock, or dewdrop. Inside, the pupa develops wings and other adult body parts, usually in two to three weeks.

When metamorphosis - the change from caterpillar to butterfly - is done, the chrysalis splits. The butterfly pulls itself out and hangs on to let its damp and wrinkled wings dry. Flexing the wings pumps blood through the veins and lets them expand. After an hour or more, the new butterfly tries them out.

One of the most amazing feats in nature is the long-distance travel or migration of millions of small butterflies over thousands of miles. Some move with the seasons. Others move when their habitat is destroyed or their food runs out. Painted ladies and monarchs are just two of the more than 200 species that migrate.

Each July, some 100 million orange-and-black monarchs begin a 3,000- to 4,000-mile journey south from Canada to milder winter climates. They've been known to fly up to 100 miles a day and reach speeds of 30 miles per hour, but a typical flight speed is ten mph. Monarchs settle along the coast in California and Baja California, and in Florida, Mexico, Central America, and Cuba. Each site has a source of fresh water and tall trees.

Before they leave Canada, monarchs fill up on nectar and store fat for their flight and the coming winter when flowers with nectar are scarce. In winter quarters, they cluster together on trees in a state of semi-hibernation at 55°F and below. Above that temperature, the sun warms their wings so that they can fly to find water or to mate.

In late February, monarchs start north. Females stop to lay up to 100 eggs each on milkweed plants. Soon after, the first generation to migrate south dies after living six to nine months. The second and third generations live six weeks each and then die. The fourth returns to Canada and produces a fifth generation, which completes the cycle by migrating south. How do monarchs know to migrate? Scientists now know that information passes from butterfly parent to child in a process called intergenerational memory. ■

Page 34: *Monarchs cluster on tall trees for warmth. Each holds tightly to a leaf with gripper feet.*

Page 35: *Moth caterpillars feed constantly.*

Aphids & kin

Aphids, cicadas, and treehoppers are all in the Homoptera, or "same wing," order. Its 45,000 species also include spittlebugs, leafhoppers, whiteflies, and scale insects. These insects don't look related, but they have common traits. Those with wings fold them like a tent. With piercing-sucking mouthparts, they feed only on plants. And all develop by simple metamorphosis.

Aphids or plant lice, probably the best-known members of the group, measure less than the height of this L. Their pear-shaped bodies take on the color of their food – yellow, red, green, or brown. Most feed on only one plant species. An aphid sticks its mouthpart into the stem and sucks out sap. What weakens and eventually kills the plant are the huge numbers of sap-suckers. If all of them survived, one female could have nearly six billion descendants.

When aphid eggs hatch in spring, the nymphs are wingless females. They give birth to live young, also wingless females. Up to 13 generations can be born in a summer without help from males, a process called parthenogenesis or virgin birth. After several generations, females with wings are born and swarm to another plant. They continue to have young until late summer or fall, when they return to the first plant. There they bear both males and females. After mating, the females lay eggs that hatch in spring.

What keeps aphids from devouring every plant in sight? Winter cold. Birds. Ladybugs, syrphid flies, lacewings, and others that lay eggs near an aphid colony. When hatched, the larvas feed on them. Lacewing larva, known as aphid-lions, can down 60 an hour. With only a sticky wax to use as a defense, aphids often rely on ants to protect them. In return, aphids give ants drops of honeydew that their bodies excrete from plant sugars.

About as big as a green pea, a treehopper can leap a distance more than 80 times its size. Its odd-shaped, colorful covering often makes it look

Two black-bodied adult treehoppers share a leaf with light-colored adults, just emerged from their last molt, and three nymphs.

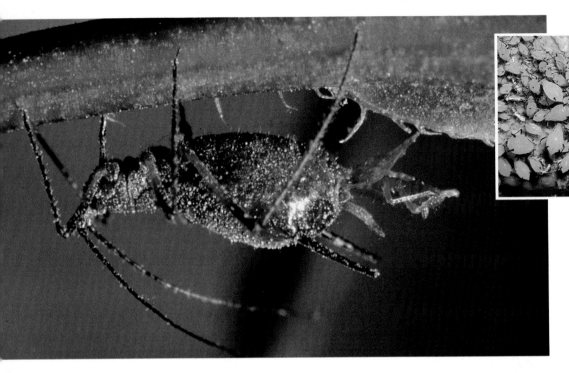

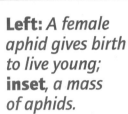

Left: *A female aphid gives birth to live young;* **inset**, *a mass of aphids.*

like a thorn or other part of plants where it feeds. Like aphids, a treehopper gives honeydew to ants. In return, it's protected from predators like spiders.

On a hot summer day, the shrill buzz of a male cicada travels a mile or more. About the size of a large peanut, it makes up to 1,000 pulses per second by moving membranes, called tymbals, in its abdomen. Like a drum, the sound vibrates in air sacs and becomes louder. After a female answers the call and the two mate, she lays eggs in slits she cuts into a tree or shrub. When it hatches, a nymph falls to the ground and burrows under with its large front legs. It eats sap from plant roots over a period of one to 17 years, depending on the species, and molts up to 30 times. Then the nymph moves above ground, climbs a tree, and splits its skin to become an adult for only a few weeks.

A cicada in the desert sweats to keep cool. When too hot, it moves water from its blood through ducts to its outer cover. No other insect is known to have these ducts. A cicada can cool itself 10 to 15 degrees below the air temperature. In 115°F heat, it uses 20 to 35 percent of its body water every hour.

Struggling out of the skin it wore as a nymph is a cicada adult.

We would die if we lost more than seven to ten percent. By keeping its cool, a cicada can feed on plants and replenish its water in full sun, while its enemies must stay in the shade. ■

Termites

Often compared with ants, termites are also social insects. Their 2,100 species live in colonies, each with a queen and often millions of workers. Termites are actually more like cockroaches than ants. Found all over the world, except polar caps, termites form the order Isoptera.

Unlike ants, termites have no pinched waist, and some workers have no eyes. Their soft bodies are often colorless. While ants have a complete metamorphosis, termites don't. At one-third inch, termite workers aren't aggressive and don't prey on other animals. Instead, a group of soldier termites with large heads and strong jaws guards and defends the nest from army ants and others. Soldiers in some species have long snouts instead of jaws. Aiming the snout like a squirt gun, a soldier shoots sticky glue on enemies.

Termites build nests in logs, buildings, and soil, hanging from trees, or as tall mounds. With their biting mouthparts, most species feed on dead wood. Colonies of microorganisms living in their intestines help them digest it. Termites gobble wood and paper at a fast rate, causing millions of dollars in property damage.

Termites tunnel from one meal to another, crawling along in darkness. The tunnels or their droppings give them away – termites leave no sawdust. In the tropics, termites can make a 100-foot-long tunnel end precisely under a log. How? Their powerful sense of smell.

Male and female termites with wings fly out into daylight during mating flights. Those not eaten by birds, bats, dragonflies, lizards, or toads break off their wings after landing. A male king and female queen dig out a small nest in the ground or in wood, seal their chamber, and mate. The first eggs become workers that care for the next broods. As an egg develops, it absorbs water until it's three times original size. The nymph that hatches looks like a miniature termite. After six molts in three months to a year, the nymph becomes an adult.

A worker termite can be male or female. It's wingless, blind, and deaf. It can live three years in a dark, damp nest. Without a hard outer shell, a termite needs moisture, or it shrivels and dies. Workers often wet parts of the nest with saliva, which evaporates and keeps it damp.

In Africa, the nest of one species can be 30 feet tall, 16 inches thick, and over 60 feet around. The mound is built to circulate air, like a central heating and air conditioning system. Compass termites in Australia control temperature by building a 15-foot-tall pyramid. A species in African rainforests builds an umbrella-shaped roof so that rain runs off. Older nests have several of these roofs and look like pagodas. Some colonies in the tropics grow fungus in old plant material as food. One colony can recycle a half ton of plant material each year. ■

A termite queen, her body swollen with eggs, may lay 10,000 a day or up to 100 million eggs during her life. Workers and large-headed soldiers feed her.

Ants

More ants live on earth than any other animal. They're everywhere. Along with bees and wasps, ants are members of the Hymenoptera order. All 1,400 species are social and live in colonies where each ant has a specific job. Largest colonies may have up to 10 million ants.

Black, brown, or reddish, ants run from microscopic to 1½ inches. Their chewing mouthparts eat plants or insects. An ant only swallows part of its food. The rest is stored in the body where it can be brought up to the mouth and fed to others in the colony, a process called trophallaxis.

With fewer than 50 lenses in its compound eyes, an ant sees poorly. It uses antennas as eyes, nose, and compass. The first ant or two out of the anthill looking for food leaves a scent trail. Others follow by touching antennas to it. How do ants recognize others in their own colony? By a one-of-a-kind group smell.

Like bees and wasps, ants store food in nests made in plants, trees, and underground. But they don't build tidy, six-sided cells because ants constantly move their food supply and young. One European ant builds a maze of underground chambers to 20 feet below ground.

Before she digs a nest, a queen ant flies into the air and mates with a male. Soon after landing, the male dies. The queen rubs or breaks off the four wings she's used only once, and her body absorbs the muscles to nourish her eggs. She feeds and tends the first set, which all hatch into workers. Nine of every ten adults is a wingless worker. Younger ones are nurses. Older ones collect food. Some clean the nest, and others defend it. Unlike a beehive, an anthill may have many queens. One leaf-cutter ant queen may lay 20 million eggs.

Nurse ants lick eggs to keep off mold and stick them together for a quick move. They also feed, clean, and carry the soft, legless larvas, called grubs, to parts of the nest where temperatures are best for them to grow. When a larva finishes growing, the

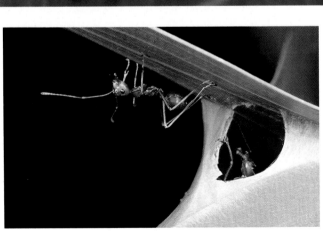

Top: *Weaver ants in Asia squeeze a larva to produce sticky silk that binds leaves into a nest,* **bottom**.

nurse ant digs a shallow pit. The larva uses silk from mouth glands to line it and spin a cocoon. At the end of 13 to 22 days when metamorphosis is complete, the nurse bites open an end of the cocoon so the new adult ant can come out.

Several animals with long, sticky tongues feed on ants: Australian numbats and echidnas, African aardvarks, Asian and African pangolins, Asian sloth bears, and South American anteaters. But ants' worst enemies are other ants. The fierce slave-making or amazon ants go into other nests and take the pupas. When mature, the captured ants must feed and care for their kidnappers.

In most parts of the world, ants are major predators, hunting insects and other animals without a backbone. Army ants swarm in huge raids. A colony of 700,000 forms a column longer than a football field and 26 feet wide. They march through the jungle killing spiders, termites, mice,

lizards, beetles, grasshoppers, and more. Prey is divided into smaller pieces to carry to their temporary nest. When these ants devour all the food in one area, they move on.

Less aggressive ants find ways to collect and store food. Harvester ants stockpile grain seeds. Leaf-cutter ants use razorlike jaws to strip a tree of leaves in one night. Each ant cuts and carries a half-inch piece of leaf to the nest, where it's chewed and added to a pile of rotting leaves. In this ant compost heap, they grow fungus for food.

Ants also get a food called honeydew from other insects, mostly aphids. Honeypot ants store honeydew in the swollen stomachs of hundreds of worker ants hanging upside down. When colony members need food, the storage ants transfer it by mouth. ■

An ant protects aphids from predators in exchange for drops of honeydew to eat.

ABOUT THE PHOTOGRAPHERS

Principal photographers **Robert and Linda Mitchell** bring their experience as educators to their photographs. Robert, an invertebrate zoologist with a Ph.D. in zoology, taught biology at Texas Tech University. Linda taught science at the elementary level. Their photos have appeared in numerous books and periodicals, including *National Geographic*, *Audubon*, and *Life*.

The Mitchell's 28 photos: pages 2 top and bottom, 3 top and bottom, 5, 7 top and bottom, 9 bottom, 10, 12, 13, 17 top and bottom, 20 top and bottom, 21, 24, 25 top, 26, 32-33, 35, 38 bottom and top inset, 39, 40 top and bottom, back cover top and bottom.

Frank Balthis: pages 16, 33 inset
Gerry Ellis: title page, pages ii-1
R. J. Erwin/DRK Photo: page 29
Michael Fogden/DRK Photo pages 10-11, 15, 36-37
Jeff Foott: page 19 bottom; with DRK Photo, page 8
Barbara Gerlach: page 31
John Gerlach/DRK Photo: page 30
Richard R. Hansen: page 34
Stephen J. Krasemann/DRK Photo: pages 4, 27 top
Dwight R. Kuhn/DRK Photo: pages 38 top left, 41
Tom and Pat Leeson/DRK Photo: pages 18, 23
Mark Moffett/Minden Pictures: pages 19 top, 27 bottom
Kevin Schafer and Martha Hill: page 28
Larry West: pages 9 top, 14, 46
Doug Wechsler: page 6 top and inset
Art Wolfe: front cover
Belinda Wright/DRK Photo: page 25 bottom

ABOUT THE AUTHOR

Insects is Joni Phelps Hunt's fifth book for Blake Books. Her previous titles are *Deserts, A Chorus of Frogs, A Shimmer of Butterflies,* and *Bears.*

SPECIAL THANKS

Gary Dunn, Young Entomologists' Society; Dr. Arthur Evans, Director, Insect Zoo, Natural History Museum of Los Angeles County; Dr. Robert Mitchell, Bandera, Texas.

TO LEARN MORE

• Ralph M. Parsons Insect Zoo, Natural History Museum, 900 Exposition Blvd., Los Angeles, CA 90007.
• SASI (Sonoran Arthropod Studies, Inc.), P.O. Box 5624, Tucson, AZ 85703.
• Xerces Society, 10 Southwest Ash St., Portland, OR 97204.
• Y.E.S. (Young Entomologists), 1915 Peggy Pl., Lansing, MI 48910.

BOOKS

• *Exploring the World of Insects – The Equinox Guide to the Behavior of Bugs,* by Adrian Forsyth (Camden House, 1992).
• *Insects of the World,* by Anthony Wooton (Facts on File Publications, 1988).
• *The Practical Entomologist: An Introductory Guide to Observing and Understanding the World of Insects,* by Rick Imes (Fireside, 1992).

FILMS

• *Backyard Bugs* (National Geographic, 1990, 15 minutes). Preschool – junior high; teacher's guide.
• *The Benefits of Insects* (National Geographic, 1990, 13 minutes). Primary grades; teacher's guide.
• *Secrets of the Ant and Insect World and Secrets of the Bee World* (Disney Educational Productions, 1990, 13 minutes). Primary – college.

WHERE TO SEE INSECT EXHIBITS

UNITED STATES

• Arthropod Discovery Center, Tucson Mountain Park, Tucson, AZ; (602) 883-3945. Open by appointment only.
• Butterfly Exhibit, San Diego Wild Animal Park, 15500 San Pasqual Rd., Escondido, CA 92027; (619) 747-8702.
• Butterfly World, Tradewinds Park, 3600 W. Sample Rd., Coconut Creek, FL 33073; (305) 977-4400.
• Butterfly World, Marine World Africa USA, Marine World Pkwy, Vallejo, CA 94589; (707) 644-4000.
• Day Butterfly Center, Callaway Gardens, Pine Mountain, GA 31822; (800) 282-8181.
• Fort Worth Zoological Park Insectarium, 1989 Colonial Pkwy., Fort Worth, TX 76110; (817) 871-7050.
• Insect World, Cincinnati Zoo and Botanical Garden, 3400 Vine St., Cincinnati, OH 45220; (513) 559-7737.
• Orkin Insect Zoo, Smithsonian Institution National Museum of Natural History, MRC 158, Washington, D.C. 20560; (202) 357-1386.
• Ralph M. Parsons Insect Zoo, Natural History Museum, 900 Exposition Blvd., Los Angeles, CA 90007; (213) 744-3558.
• San Francisco Zoological Society Insect Zoo, 45th Ave. and Sloat Blvd., San Francisco, CA 94132; (415) 753-7053.

CANADA

• The Insectarium of Montreal, Montreal Botanical Garden, 4581 Sherbrooke, Montreal, Quebec H1X 2B2; (514) 872-8753.
• Butterfly World, P.O. Box 36, Coombs, British Columbia V0R 1M0; (604) 248-7026.

GLOSSARY

INDEX

CLOSE-UP
A Focus on Nature

Here's what teachers, parents, kids, and nature lovers of all ages say about this series:

• • • • • • • •

"High-interest topics, written in grownup language yet clear enough for kids..."

"Dazzling, detailed photos. Your beautiful books have a strong educational component—keep it up!"

"Packed with facts and priced right for busy adults."

"Extremely useful for students with reading difficulties..."

"Your book is the best souvenir we could have of our whale-watching trip."

"These books are great gift items for all the bird-watchers, divers, and wildlife artists on my list!"

Silver Burdett Press books are widely available at bookstores and gift outlets at museums, zoos, and aquaria throughout the U.S. and abroad. Educators and individuals wishing to order may also do so by writing directly to:

SILVER BURDETT PRESS
299 JEFFERSON ROAD,
PARSIPPANY, NJ 07054

◆ HABITATS ◆

- The **Desert** — Hot & dry, but it's home to big cats, camels, coyotes, & more
- The **KELP FOREST** — The ebb and flow of life in the sea's richest habitat
- **Life at the Frozen Edge** — **ICEBERGS AND GLACIERS**
- Tropical **RAINFOREST**
- **Coral Reef**
- **Tidepools** — The bright world of the rocky shoreline

◆ BIRDS ◆
IN THE WILD

- HAWKS, OWLS & OTHER **Birds of Prey**
- **PARROTS, MACAWS & COCKATOOS**
- A dazzle of **Hummingbirds**

◆ ANIMALS ◆
BIG & SMALL

- **BEARS**
- **Insects** — All about ants, aphids, bees, fleas, termites, toebiters, & a beetle or two
- A CHORUS OF **FROGS**
- **ELEPHANTS**
- 165 million years of **DINOSAURS**
- **Butterflies** — Monarchs, moths & more — up close & unexpected

◆ MARINE LIFE ◆

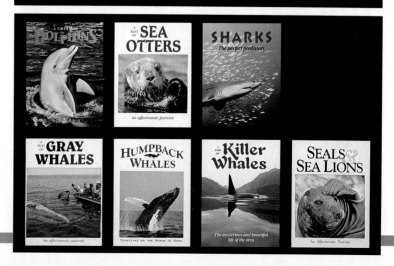

- A CHORUS OF **DOLPHINS**
- A RAFT OF **SEA OTTERS** — An affectionate portrait
- **SHARKS** — The perfect predators
- A POD OF **GRAY WHALES** — An affectionate portrait
- **HUMPBACK WHALES** — Traveling on the wings of song
- A POD OF **Killer Whales** — The mysterious and beautiful life of the orca
- **SEALS & SEA LIONS** — An Affectionate Portrait